Zen for Cats

Zen for Cats

Teachings of the Zen Cat Masters

as intuited by
Alfred Birnbaum and Riku Kanmei

illustrations by J.C. Brown

New York • WEATHERHILL • Tokyo

First edition, 1993

Published by Weatherhill, Inc.
420 Madison Avenue, 15th Floor
New York, N.Y. 10017

Printed in the U.S.A.

96   95   94   93   8   7   6   5   4   3   2   1

Library of Congress Cataloging-in-Publication Data

Birnbaum, Alfred.
    Zen for cats / by Alfred Birnbaum & Riku Kanmei illustrations by
J.C. Brown.
       p.   cm.
    ISBN 0-8348-0275-9. $9.95
    1. Cats—Humor.   2. Zen Buddhism—Humor.   3. Wit and humor.
Pictorial.   I. Kanmei, Riku.   II. Brown, J.C.   III. Title.
PN6231.C23B57   1993
818'.5402—dc20   92-46104
                                                             CIP

Contents

Zen For Cats

The Tail of

the Teachings

Words are but paw-prints

The Scriptures are mere tracks, leading us across the carpet toward the sunniest spot on the floor—they are not the cat lying in the sunlight.

Cats in their wisdom know that Knowledge only scratches at Truth, and Enlightenment is meaningless without a compassionate lap to enjoy it on. So if they seem to freely bestow their not-quite-so-humble teachings on us humans, the truth is, cats want something from us along the Way.

4

Host or Guest?

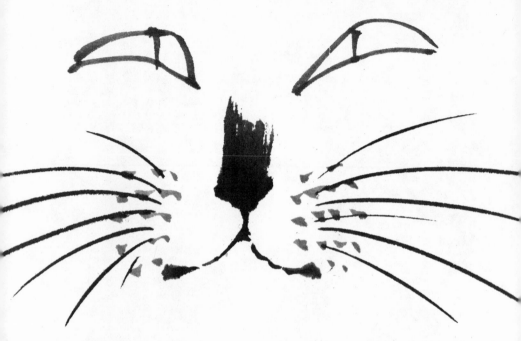

Whether sleeping, stretching, or gazing out the window, cats never cease to look within, realizing that enlightenment is closer than the tip of one's nose. As the oft-quoted koan goes:

Pink nose, black nose—not-two

Cat Zen began in ancient India, two-and-a-half millennia ago. A furry pilgrim named Mahakatsya journeyed from afar to hear the Buddha preach, but found him fast asleep. Puzzled, the seeker gave the World-Honored One a respectful bat on the nose. The Awakened One opened his Dharma Eyes and smiled at Mahakatsya, and in a blinding flash the cat attained Enlightenment. Whereupon the Selfless Snooze became a core practice of *Fur-Footed Buddhism*.

Ten centuries later, Bodhipurrma, the scruffy First Patriarch of Cat Zen, carried the fleas of Non-Attachment over the Himalayas from India. This tough old tomcat then sat facing a mousehole in meditation for nine years—so long, in fact, that he was mistaken for a throwrug. Ever since, the Zen cat has followed the strict practice of contemplative sitting and ritual purrrification by licking.

Still later, the High-Strung Blue-Point Master Fe-Lien established a warm place in the Imperial Court of the Sung dynasty. In China, Cat Zen became known for its ineffable expressions of "thusness"—basking, rolling, yawning, napping, nibbling, and romping. As Master Fe-Lien instructed:

The tabby knows where to grow stripes

9

Eventually, lured by the aroma of raw fish, Cat Zen crossed the sea and arrived in Japan. Here the sect achieved its greatest refinement, under the erratic guidance of the Bob-Tailed Master D.T. Sushi Roshi. His disciples went on to create the catnip ceremony, the One-Slash School of Sofa Shredding, and other arts close to the heart of Japanese culture. Soon, behind every successful haiku poet was a cat:

An old futon
Tora jumps on
The sound of the hours

BASHO   TORA

11

Cat Zen offers vital truths for all sentient beings. But be forewarned: The Teachings are universal but unfathomable, both rigorous and subtle. When in doubt, consult your own little spiritual master. Pose the age-old question to any pointed ear:

Does a Buddha have Cat-Nature?

The answer: an unequivocal

oonww!!

Meditation

Contemplating the here and now

(until mealtime)

On Ceaseless Change
"All sitcoms are impermanent"

On Transmigration
Same ingredients, different vessels

On the One and the Many

What's a Zen cat to do?

On Transcendence

The Master sees what we can't

On Human Concerns

And ignores what we can

On the Scriptures

Hard is the seat of wisdom

On Emptiness

Easy is the vow of poverty

On Chaos

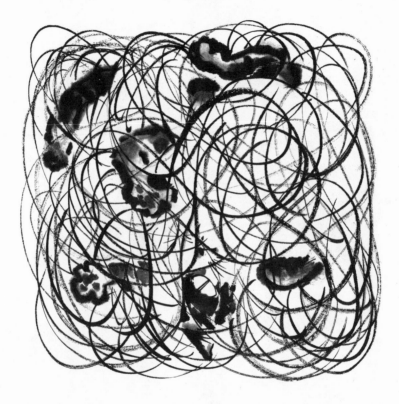

The immutable Law of Paws and Effect

On Cycles

Born to be wild

On the Sutras

Namrrr Sakyrrrrmmunnrrrr Buddhrrr

On Desire

Fur burns

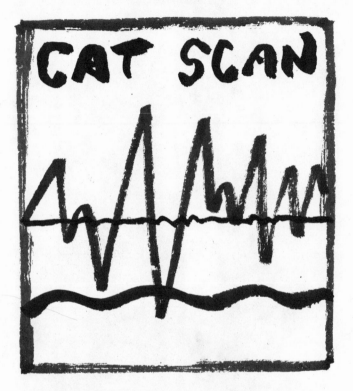

More waves than one to scan a cat

On Cholesterol

What color is your prosciutto?

On Appearances

I sniff what you think

On Death

"Where is thy wing?"

On Nature

Becoming one with small living creatures

On second thought, staying indoors

It rains outside all windows

Kat Koans

What is the sound

of one can opening?

Door open—Stay in!
Door closed—Go out!

34

Roll in dirt, get clean

Find where paths cross—

Sit smack center

Don't bother the Buddha—

     I'm eating

Don't bother the Buddha—

     I'm sleeping

Don't bother the Buddha—

     I don't want to be bothered

39

Zen today, Zen tomorrow

Eat and sleep—

Nothing sacred about the Order

One coat of fur sheds everywhere

Steak and hamburger are the same—
Only the names are different

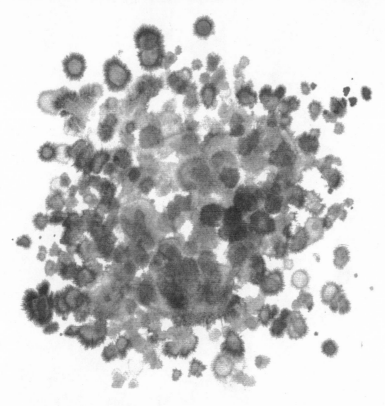

Gulp it down—No good!

Throw it up—No good!

45

Enter the den of the tiger—

Stroke its whiskers

Clawing the keeper's treasures

The bird does not ask to be stalked

Fluff is void, void is fluff

If I have but nine lives to live,

let me live them as a cat

Knocking at the Gate

Acknowledging the Master

CATS
MUST
WASH
PAWS!

Washing the Feet

Taking the Vows

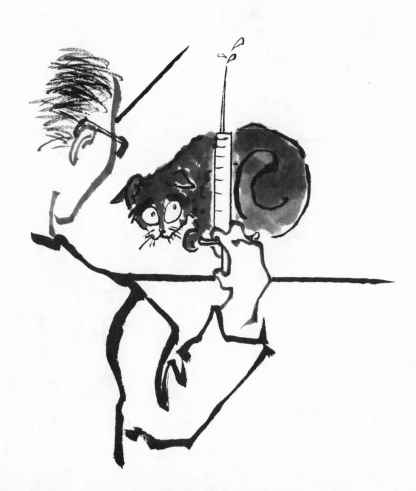

Accepting the Teachings

Wandering and Begging

Taking Refuge in the Brotherhood

Renouncing the Lay Life

Attainment

Zen Fish, Zen Bones

A cautionary tale of

the perils of the worldly life

Raw Fish

Smoked Fish

Grilled Fish

Canned Fish

Fried Fish

Raking Sand

Seasonal patterns in the box garden

Dig with the mind

Not with the feet

Concentrate

Leave not a trace

The Ten Sacred
String-Chasing

On the impermanence of common

Pictures

household objects

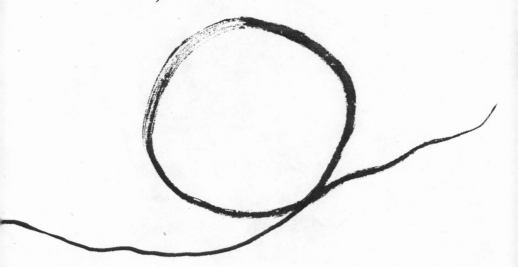

1

Looking for the String

In the living room of this world,
Lost amidst the interpenetrating paths,
I see only bobby pins and dustballs.
Unamused, I can find no String.

2

Sensing the Movement

Distant as the back hall, do I hear footsteps?
A drawer opens on untold mysteries!
I stand at the threshold with whiskers awakened.
Traces are everywhere, at the end of my nose.

3

Turning the Corner

Where, oh where does this path lead?
I seek my way through God-knows-what all.
Curiosity aroused, no door can contain me,
Nowhere the String can hide!

4

Over

Rising to the occasion, I jump the teak bureau.
Perilous are the Lemon-Pledged heights—
The lamp cord is but a shadow of the String
And the light that falls is not the Light.

5

Under

Swept beneath the rug of existence,
The myriad things shine like stray cufflinks.
Lured through the loop of delusion's purse strap,
I lose the String along with kitsch.

6

Sideways

Tangled in the fabric of non-being,
I merge with the lint of the ages.
The knot is tied, but not the String—
This silken slip isn't out of the bag.

7

Down

Light, more light, I scoot beyond the folds,
These veils of illusion that drape and blind.
I draw the curtain on this chintzy play
And sever all ties, no String attached.

8

String Gone, Cat Gone

String and self both transcended,
A great stillness pervades all quarters,
Like calm after a passing storm—
It's so quiet you can hear a priceless antique drop.

9

Cat Bored

No truth to gain, nowhere to go,
I sharpen my claws on blissful repose.
If a hundred birds strew my path with Friskies,
In one yawn I would swallow them all.

10

Entering the Kitchen

No pussyfooting here, my paws to refresh,
I rub against the Master's legs.
Blessings on the Buddhas of the Six Supermarkets—
Spirituality really works up an appetite!

Satori

" Enlightenment

beyond words

The "weathermark" identifies this book as a production of Weatherhill, Inc, publishers of fine books on Asia and the Pacific. Typography, book, and cover design: Liz Trovato. Production supervision: Bill Rose. Typesetting: Trufont Typographers, Hicksville, N.Y. Printing and binding: Kingsport Press, Kingsport, Tennessee. The typefaces used are Diotima for text and Present for display.